WORLD FAITHS

HINDUISM

AND OTHER

EASTERN RELIGIONS

All year dates are given using the Christian conventions B.C. (Before Christ) and A.D. (Anno Domini), simply for universality of understanding

The publishers would like to thank the following editorial consultants for their help:
Dr. Stewart McFarlane, visiting professor at Chung Hwa Institute of Buddhist Studies, Taiwan
Dr. Eleanor Nesbitt, Lecturer in Religions and Education, University of Warwick, England
Ranchor Prime, member of the International Consultancy on Religion, Education, and Culture
Shaunka Rishi Das, Director of the Oxford Centre for Hindu Studies, England
Inderjit Singh, editor of the *Sikh Messenger*

KINGFISHER
LONDON & NEW YORK

Published in the United States by Kingfisher,
175 Fifth Ave., New York, NY 10010
Kingfisher is an imprint of Macmillan Children's Books, London.

Distributed in the U.S. and Canada by Macmillan, 175 Fifth Ave., New York, NY 10010

First published as *The Kingfisher Book of Religions* in 1999
This revised and updated edition published in 2013

LIBRARY OF CONGRESS CATALOGING-IN-PUBLICATION DATA
HAS BEEN APPLIED FOR

ISBN 978-0-7534-6912-5

Kingfisher books are available for special promotions and premiums.
For details contact: Special Markets Department, Macmillan,
175 Fifth Ave., New York, NY 10010

For more information, please visit www.kingfisherbooks.com

Printed in China
2 4 6 8 10 9 7 5 3 1
1TR/1112/UTD/WKT/128MA

WORLD FAITHS

HINDUISM

AND OTHER

EASTERN RELIGIONS

Worship, festivals, and ceremonies from around the world

TREVOR BARNES

KINGFISHER
NEW YORK

CONTENTS

INTRODUCTION

Above *Here, a yoga class takes place on a beach in Cape Town, South Africa. Ancient religious practices of the East are becoming increasingly attractive to people from Western cultures wanting to develop their spiritual awareness.*

Some religions believe in one God who created the Earth and everything in it. Others have several gods who take many forms and influence human lives in sometimes surprising ways. And while, for example, Buddhists and Jains do not generally believe in God at all, other believers prefer to refer to a higher power or life force that creates and sustains all things.

But what most religions have in common is the idea of transcendence—that there are more things in life than those we can understand with our minds or experience with our senses. The spiritual dimension to existence—that is to say the mysterious, powerful, and invisible force in this life (and beyond)—is at the heart of all the world's major religions.

Prehistoric religion

The prehistoric era is the massive period of time before written records appeared. It stretches from the beginning of humankind more than two million years ago to the development of writing in the ancient civilizations of the Middle East some 5,000 years ago.

Since no written explanations of prehistoric religions exist, we have to rely on archaeological evidence to put the pieces of the religious jigsaw puzzle together. Huge stones, or megaliths, like those in Stonehenge in southern England suggest some sort of religious worship, as do graves and burial mounds, carved idols, and the remains of altars. Precious objects, like swords, chariots, jewels, and even boats discovered in tombs housing the dead, suggest that our ancestors believed in an afterlife in which all these artifacts would be of use to the dead person throughout eternity.

Right *Every year more than one million pilgrims travel to Hinduism's holiest city, Venares, to bathe in the waters of the sacred Ganges River and receive its blessings.*

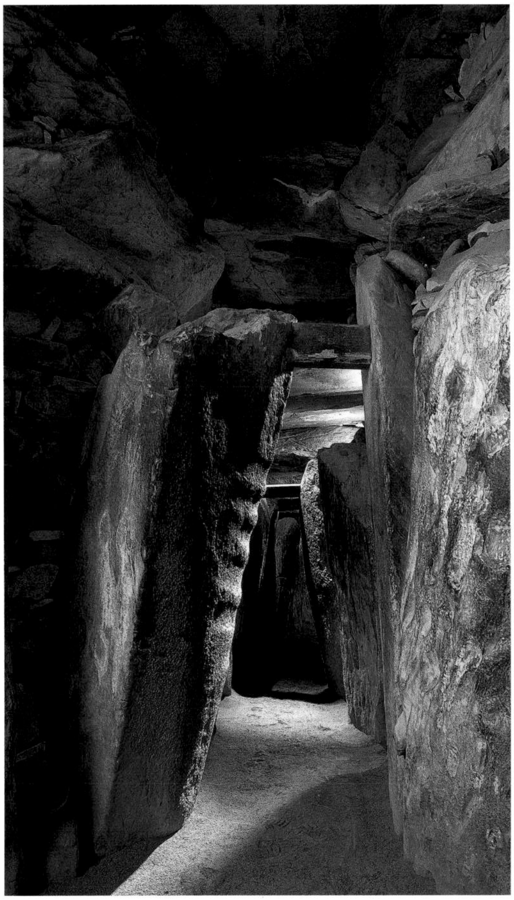

Hinduism—the eternal truth

For our ancestors, such as those living by the Indus River in modern-day Pakistan more than 5,000 years ago, nature was a powerful force in their lives. It was common for them to look to it for protection and reassurance.

These forces were eventually associated with individual gods who were believed to possess superhuman powers to create life or destroy it. People told stories and recited poems about them, not only for entertainment but also to help understand the origin and purpose of Creation. In this way the most ancient of the world's living faiths—Hinduism—was born. Hindus, however, do not believe that their religion had a beginning. For them it is a truth that exists and has existed throughout the unending cycles of time.

Their wisdom was eventually written down in the ancient language of Sanskrit and formed the basis of the Hindu scriptures, which are an inspiration to the estimated 800 million Hindu believers in the world today.

The appeal of Eastern religion today

Eastern religions often appeal to people looking for direct spiritual experience. They argue that religions such as Judaism, Christianity, and Islam rely too heavily on rules and regulations. Instead they look to the Eastern traditions of meditation and contemplation to take them beyond words into a mystical world of the spirit—a world where God can be felt and perceived.

Above *The passage grave of Newgrange, Ireland, is 5,000 years old. On the shortest day of the year it is briefly illuminated by the rays of the rising Sun. Could this be evidence of a prehistoric belief in the power of light over darkness?*

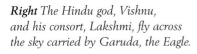

Right *The Hindu god, Vishnu, and his consort, Lakshmi, fly across the sky carried by Garuda, the Eagle.*

THE ORIGINS OF HINDUISM

Hinduism has its origins in the civilization that developed some 4,500 years ago along the Indus Valley, a corridor of fertile land stretching from the Himalayas through present-day Pakistan to the Arabian Sea. This civilization flourished from *c.*2500–B.C. 1500, and produced a highly developed culture centered on two cities: Mohenjo-Daro and Harappa.

Early history

Archaeological excavations made in 1921 revealed that these cities, the first on the Indian subcontinent, were enormous in size and elaborate in construction. The streets were laid out in a grid pattern and the buildings were solid with high defenses. What also came to light were numerous clay figurines depicting a mother goddess. She seems to have been worshiped as a source of life and creation and is a forerunner of the mother goddess Mahadevi in classical Hinduism.

The Vedic period

Some scholars claim that around 1500 B.C., tribes of Aryan people from the Caucasus region of Central Asia invaded the Indus Valley and the northwest plains of the Indian subcontinent. They brought with them their traditions and their language (which later became Sanskrit) and mixed elements of their own culture with the existing culture of the Indus Valley. Others say that it was development within the tradition, not invasion by an outside force, that brought about changes to the religion.

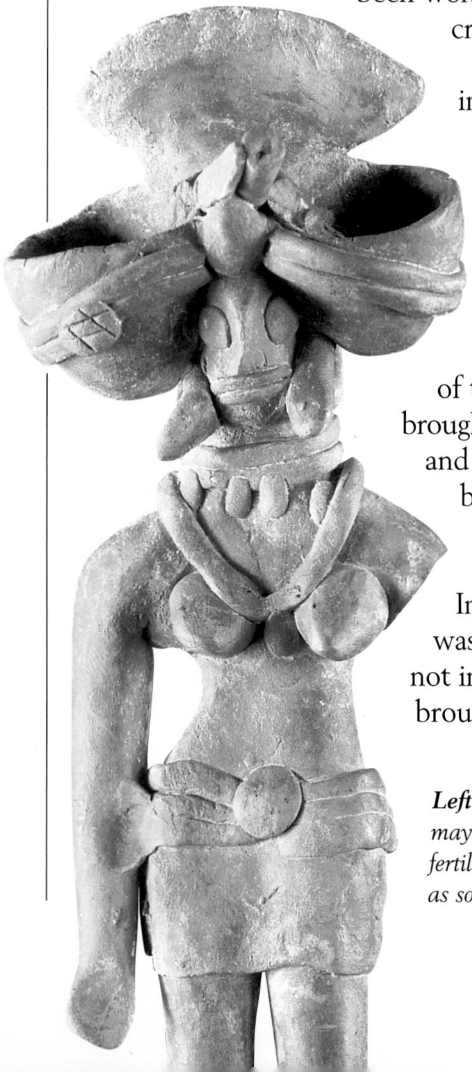

Left *This terracotta model from Mohenjo-Daro may be of the mother goddess, who represented life, fertility, and the fruits of the Earth. She was worshiped as someone who provided and cared for humankind.*

A typical Harrapan house had an open courtyard. Thick, windowless walls kept the inside of the house cool.

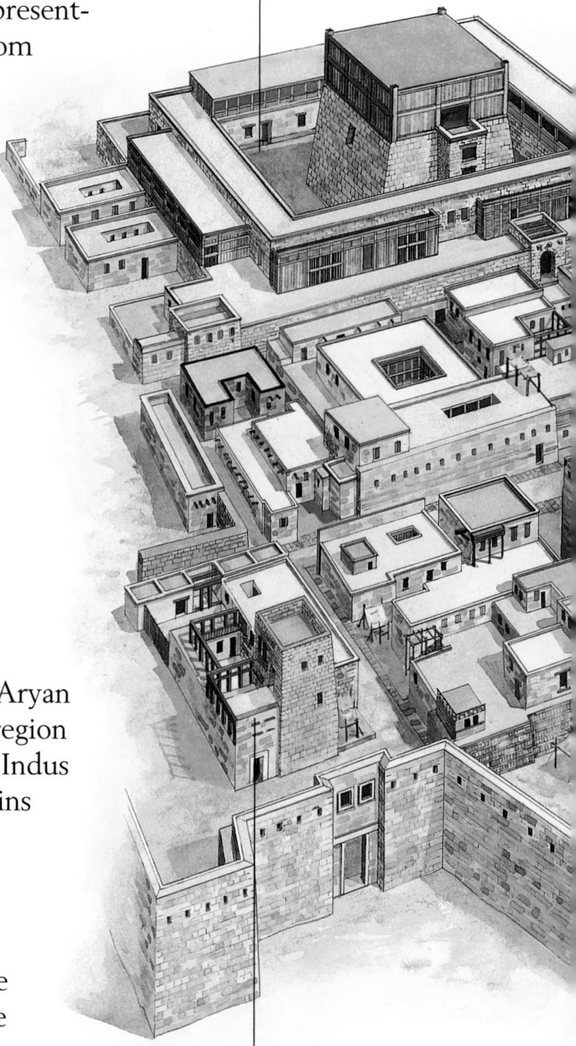

The brick houses had a sophisticated drainage system, and many had grain storerooms.

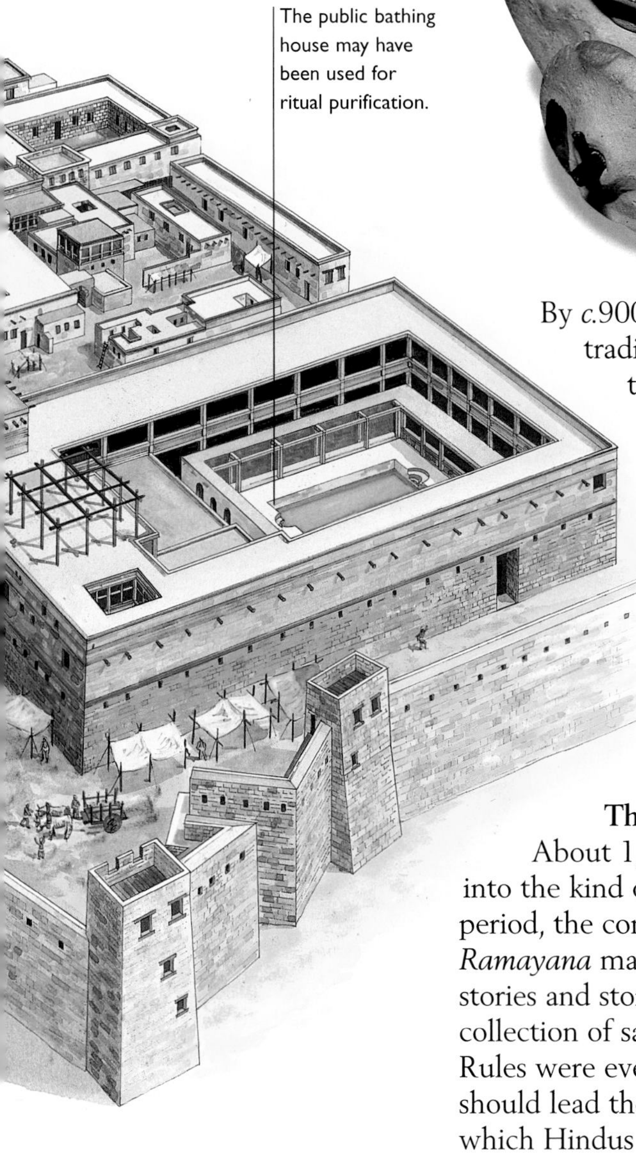

The public bathing house may have been used for ritual purification.

Below *At its peak, Mohenjo-Daro had a population of around 30,000. Many of the buildings were made of baked bricks—and the bricks were made to a uniform size.*

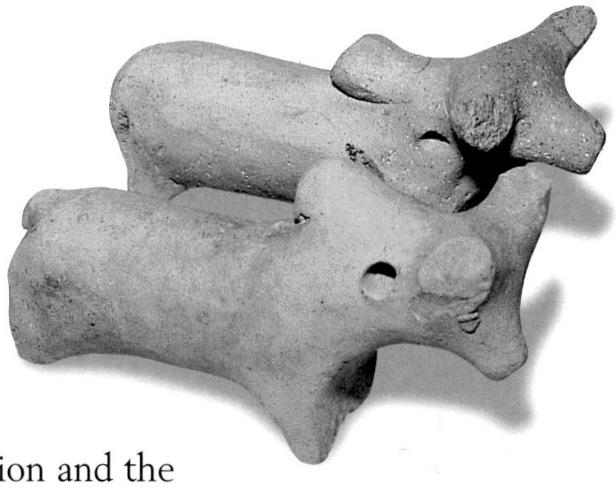

Below *This model chariot with bullocks was found in Harappa. Such artifacts suggest that this was an increasingly sophisticated civilization that recognized a connection between the natural and the spiritual worlds.*

By *c.*900 B.C., the oral tradition had given way to the written tradition and the religious beliefs were put into writing in the form of the sacred texts we know as the four *Vedas* (*see* page 38). The Vedic religion that developed during this period is based on the ritual sacrifice of animals to many different gods, especially Indra, the god of war and storms, and Agni, the god of fire. Vedic gods have much in common with ancient Greek and Roman gods, who also represented the elements and the forces of nature.

The *Puranas*

About 1,800 years ago, religious ideas and practices crystallized into the kind of Hinduism broadly recognized today. During this period, the completion of the epic poems the *Mahabharata* and the *Ramayana* marked a cultural and religious step forward. Creation stories and stories about the lives of the gods appeared in another collection of sacred texts, known as the *Puranas* (*see* pages 38–39). Rules were eventually drawn up to govern the way that Hindus should lead their lives. These included four stages, or *ashramas,* which Hindus should ideally experience if they are to reach *moksha*—liberation from the ongoing cycle of birth, death, and rebirth. The four stages are: being a student to learn about the sacred literature; being a householder to develop responsibility in society; being a contemplative to reflect and meditate on important things in life; and being an ascetic and to renounce the pleasures of the world.

HINDU GODS AND GODDESSES

Hindus believe in one god as the ultimate source of reality and existence. They describe their god as Brahman, the unseen, all-powerful force responsible for bringing all creation into being, and to which all creation will ultimately return. Brahman is neutral and impersonal and has to be approached through a series of personal deities, both male and female. The principal deities are Brahma, Vishnu, Shiva, and the goddess Mahadevi, but there are many other gods. These include gods from the Vedic period.

Below *Ganesh, the Remover of Obstacles, is the elephant-headed deity very popular with children. Ganesh is often honored at the start of a journey. Traditionally, he is very fond of candy and most statues to him show him holding some candy in his hand.*

Right *Hanuman is the clever monkey god who came to the aid of Rama when he was fighting the demon, Ravana, King of Lanka. Hanuman is worshiped as a source of protection.*

The deities from this period represent the forces of nature and include Agni, Indra, and Varuna. Agni is the god of fire and the life force of nature. Varuna maintains the cosmic order, has the power to punish and reward, and is worshiped as god of the waters and oceans. Indra is the god of the sky and the rain. These gods are addressed in the thousand or so hymns that make up the sacred text known as the *Rig Veda* (*see* page 38).

In addition to the main gods, there are lesser gods such as Vayu, the god of wind, and Surya, the god of the sun. Hindus believe that there are elements of the divine in all living things, so particular animals are worshiped as part of the divine plan. In four of his incarnations, the god Vishnu assumes the form of an animal. He appears as a fish, a tortoise, a boar, and a man-lion.

Two other gods that are particularly important in Hindu worship are Hanuman, the monkey god, and Ganesh, one of the two sons of Shiva. Ganesh is a very popular god in India. It is said that following a misunderstanding, Ganesh's father, Shiva, accidentally beheaded him. When he realized his mistake, he was so upset that he promised to replace his head with the head of the first living thing he saw —which happened to be an elephant. Ganesh, who is known as the Remover of Obstacles, and is worshiped as the god of learning, is portrayed with a human body (with a large pot belly!) and an elephant's head with one tusk. Hindus often have a favorite deity and may have a special shrine in the home.

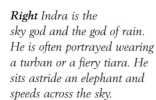

Right *Indra is the sky god and the god of rain. He is often portrayed wearing a turban or a fiery tiara. He sits astride an elephant and speeds across the sky.*

The Sacred Writings

The earliest of the Hindu scriptures are the four texts known collectively as the *Vedas*, which were begun before B.C. 1000. They are the first examples of Hindu written tradition. The oldest of the *Vedas* is the *Rig Veda*, which contains more than 1,000 hymns written in Sanskrit and is addressed to the elemental gods of Earth, fire, air, and water.

Much later, an important collection of philosophical works known as the *Upanishads* appeared. These try to explain the meaning of existence and to provide answers to the big questions in life, such as where we come from, why we are here, and what will happen to us when we die. The *Vedas* and the *Upanishads* are regarded as the revealed words of God and not a single syllable of them can be changed. In addition to a collection known as the *Puranas*, which contains stories of the lives and adventures of the gods, there are two other important works of Hindu literature, called the *Mahabharata* and the *Ramayana*.

Above *A chariot fight takes place between Bhima and Arjuna, two Pandava brothers, and Drona, leader of the opposing forces.*

The *Mahabharata*

The *Mahabharata* was written in its present form between 300 and 100 B.C. and is probably the largest single poem in the world, containing about 200,000 lines. This epic poem tells the story of the war between the five Pandava brothers, helped by their distant relative Krishna, and their 100 cousins, who live in Kurukshetra, near what is now Delhi. The war, caused by a dispute over who is the rightful ruler, is long and bitter. Although the five brothers eventually win, the story gains its power from the different attitudes shown by the brothers to the realities of fighting. For example, the third brother, called Arjuna, is a superb fighter and commander, but objects to warfare. As the story unfolds, the reader is presented with discussions about every aspect of Hindu life, including its laws, politics, geography, astronomy, and science. Consequently, what emerges alongside an exciting story of warfare is a kind of textbook of Hindu thinking.

"These words of glory to the God who is light shall be words supreme among things that are great. I glorify Varuna almighty, the god who is loving toward him who adores. We praise you with our thoughts, O God. We praise you as the sun praises you in the morning; may we find joy in being your servants."

Extract from the *Rig Veda* in honor of Varuna, the upholder of the cosmic order

Above *The* Ramayana *is more than 50,000 lines long, and was written down around 200* B.C. *It tells the adventures of Prince Rama of Ayodhya, seen here sitting with his brothers and companions, having rescued his wife Sita from the clutches of Ravana, the ten-headed demon king of Lanka.*

The Bhagavad Gita

A central section of the *Mahabharata* is known as the *Bhagavad Gita* (the Song of the Lord). It is a conversation between Arjuna and his charioteer (who is none other than Krishna, the incarnation of Vishnu), but it also explores the essential questions of life. It is a meditation on the nature of God and an exploration of the ways of achieving liberation (*moksha*) through work, devotion, and knowledge. If the *Mahabharata* is sometimes described as an encyclopedia of Hindu life, the 18 chapters that make up the Bhagavad Gita are often regarded as the "bible" of Hinduism.

Right *Om is the sacred word for god and is repeated in* mantra, *or prayers. Its deep humming sound is supposed to be a living contact with the divine presence.*

THE HINDU TRINITY

The Hindu idea of God is contained in the word *Brahman*, which means “the origin and the cause of all existence.” Brahman appears to humans in various forms and is worshiped in the shape of different gods and goddesses. Chief among these are three male gods: Brahma, Vishnu, and Shiva—the Hindu Trinity. Brahma is the creator who brings the universe into existence; Vishnu preserves life and all living things; Shiva is the destroyer (also known as the Lord of Time), who destroys the world. This ongoing cycle of creation, preservation, and destruction is at the center of Hindu belief. There is no real end or beginning to life. The beginning is an end and the end is a new beginning.

***Above** Brahma sits upon the lotus from which he was born at the time of creation. His wife is Sarasvati, the goddess of learning.*

Brahma the creator

Since Brahma is the lord of all creation, he is considered to be above human worship and very few temples are dedicated to him. When he is shown in paintings and carvings, he is often seen with four faces and four arms, and sometimes on a swan or a lotus flower.

***Above** A group of young Indian women pray in front of a shrine representing the Hindu mother goddess, Mahadevi.*

Vishnu the preserver

Vishnu is responsible for controlling human fate. He appears in ten incarnations, or *avatars*. The two most important are Krishna, the most popular god, and Rama. Vishnu is often portrayed riding majestically across the heavens on an eagle (Garuda). In his hand, he may hold a discus, symbolizing the sun, or a mace, suggesting the power of nature.

***Below** Shiva the destroyer dances in a circle of fire. At his feet lies a demon he has killed.*

Matsya the fish saved humanity from the flood.
Kurma the turtle carried the world on his back.
Varaha the boar raised the Earth with his tusks.
Narasimha, half-man and half-lion, defeated evil demons.
Vamana the dwarf defeated demons.
Krishna is renowned as a warrior, a teacher, and a lover.
Rama fights against evil in the world and upholds virtue and law.
Parasurama (Rama with an axe) defeated the warrior caste.
Kalki, who will appear riding a white horse, is yet to come.
Buddha is "the enlightened one" and the founder of Buddhism.

Above *The protective power of Vishnu (shown in the center of the picture in the form of Krishna with his consort Radha) appears on Earth in ten incarnations, or* avatars, *which prevent evil in the world.*

Shiva the destroyer

Shiva is a god in whom all opposites meet and are resolved into one. So, while Shiva is believed to be responsible for destroying creation, he is also thought to be responsible for re-creating it. Shiva's wife appears in many forms, each representing an aspect of his character. Kali is fierce and is depicted surrounded by skulls or carrying severed heads and limbs. Parvati is known for her kindness and gentleness and is often shown with her son Ganesh, who has an elephant's head and one tusk.

Hindu Worship

Daily worship is known as *puja* and for most Hindus is usually carried out in the home. A shrine richly decorated with pictures or statues (*murtis*) of favorite gods is set aside for this purpose. Wealthier families sometimes set aside a whole room as a shrine and worship there individually or as a family. *Puja* begins with the simplest but most important prayer (*mantra*)—the saying of the sacred word *Om* to make contact with the divine. This is followed by the recitation of other *mantras* from the scriptures and the offering of gifts (candy, money, fruit, etc.) to a particular god.

Worship is also carried out in the temple (*mandir*) under the supervision of a high-caste priest, or *Brahmin*. Although Hindus believe that their god is everywhere, they also believe that the temple is his special home. Only the priest is allowed to come close to the divine presence which "resides" in the inner sanctuary of the building, in the holy of holies known as the *garbhagriha* (womb-house).

Above *Children light candles to celebrate Diwali, the festival of lights.*

Below *Women pray in a Hindu temple on the Indonesian island of Bali.*

Above The Dusserah festival takes place in September or October. Effigies are burned in a reenactment of the triumph of Rama, Lakshman, and Hanuman over the demon Ravana, recorded in the epic Ramayana.

Before worship begins, members of the congregation carry out elaborate rituals of purification, which may involve washing the feet, rinsing the mouth, or preparing special food. The priest leads the worship by reading from the sacred texts and saying *mantras*. Small devotional lamps (*divas*) are lit, and after worship, the people share the food that has been blessed and offered to the gods.

"Lights are lit in Hindu households to guide Lakshmi, the goddess of fortune, into the home."

From the *Mahabharata*

Making a pilgrimage

Pilgrimage is an important part of Hindu worship and involves making the effort to travel to a sacred site. As such, it is considered an act of worship in itself. Particularly holy are sites associated with the birth or life of a god, such as Ayodhya, the legendary birthplace of Lord Rama; Kurukshetra, where the great war described in the *Mahabharata* is said to have taken place; Varanasi, also known as "the city of light," and believed to be the home of Lord Shiva; and Mathura, the birthplace of Lord Krishna. In addition, many Hindus will make a special journey to fords (safe crossing places in rivers). These symbolize the crossing from one life to another and the transition from *samsara* to *moksha* (*see* page 33), which every devout Hindu hopes to make. The most sacred river in India is the Ganges, named after Ganga, the river goddess. Bathing in its waters is an act of devotion, and bathing at the pilgrimage site of Varanasi is thought to be particularly special.

Hindu Festivals

March **Holi:** the festival (*left*) when people from all backgrounds mingle and throw colored powder (symbolizing fertility) over each other. It is celebrated with bonfires and street parties.
Shivaratri: a national celebration honoring Shiva.

August **Janmashtami:** the birthday of Krishna.

September **Dusserah:** celebrating the triumph of good over evil.
Ganesh Chaturthi: the birthday of Ganesh.

October **Diwali:** the festival of lights in honor of Rama's safe return from exile.

JAIN BELIEF AND WORSHIP

Jains do not believe in one god, nor do they pray to gods to help them. Instead, they rely on spiritual teachers to train them in meditation and self-discipline, which will enable them to be released from the prison of day-to-day existence into the joy of ultimate liberation. Ordinary Jains, as well as monks and nuns, practice asceticism because they believe that only through controlling natural desires and appetites can a person be free of the material world. Central to this belief is the concept of *karma*, which is different from that of the Hindus and Buddhists (*see* pages 45 and 59). For Jains, *karma* is composed of fine particles that stick to the soul, like mud sticks to a shoe, gradually building up and weighing it down. Doing bad deeds creates heavy *karma*, which prevents the soul's liberation, but doing good deeds causes the *karma* to be washed away, eventually allowing the liberated soul (*siddha*) to rise up to the heights of the universe, where it can live forever in spiritual freedom.

Above *This typically ornate carving is from the 14th-century Jain temple of Chaumukha.*

Right *Jain temples are beautiful works of architecture, often richly decorated and carved to show reverence for the sacred images (*pujas*) of the* Tirthankaras *placed inside. This one is in the Indian state of Gujarat. Worship may involve quiet meditation or the repetition of a* mantra *(a word or syllable believed to possess spiritual power). The worshiper may also decorate an image with flowers or anoint it with special liquids.*

Sources of *karma*

Jains believe that the principal sources of *karma* are: attachment to possessions and the material things in life; the expression of anger, pride, deceit, or greed; and false belief. The rejection of material things can be used to the advantage of others, and Jains are known for their charitable giving and the way they use their wealth to build temples, hospitals, and schools. Jains are encouraged to strengthen their devotional life by setting aside 48 minutes every day in which to practice meditation and to live one complete day as a monk during the major festival of Pajjusana.

Below *Many Jains have a shrine in their home for daily worship. They rise before dawn and invoke the Five Supreme Beings, who represent stages along the path to spiritual liberation.*

Sikhism's Ten Gurus

The development of Sikhism is inseparable from the lives of the Ten Gurus who shaped the religion over the first two centuries of its existence. The religion was founded by Guru Nanak in the A.D. 1400s, when he began to attract a group of followers who wanted a simpler, purer form of devotion, uncluttered by ritual. Originally, the group led an intensely spiritual life, meditating on the name of God and singing the devotional hymns Nanak had written. They lived a communal life and followed three basic rules: *kirt karo* (hard work); *nam japo* (worship of the Divine Name); and *vand cauko* (sharing the fruits of their labors).

Above *Guru Gobind Singh is surrounded by his sons. He was the last of the living gurus, and is chiefly remembered for founding the Khalsa and for his decision to treat the Sikh holy scripture as if it were itself a living guru.*

A succession of gurus

Nanak's successor was Guru Angad (1504–1552), who is chiefly remembered for composing the Gurmukhi script in which the Punjabi language was written down for worship. The third guru was Amar Das (1479–1574), who founded the town of Goindval in Punjab, where Sikhs gathered twice a year to renew friendships and to deepen their faith. The fourth guru, Guru Ram Das (1534–1581), moved the Sikh's spiritual center from Goindval to what is now Amritsar. The fifth guru, Guru Arjan (1563–1606), was the son of Guru Ram Das, who built the Golden Temple. The Sikhs' next leader, Guru Hargobind (1595–1644), transformed the community (the *Panth*) into a more militant force. Guru Har Rai (1630–1661) was the seventh Guru. He was followed by Har Krishan (1656–64) and then by Guru Tegh Bahadur (1621–1675) and Guru Gobind Singh (1666–1708).

Left *This Sikh is being initiated into the Khalsa (community of the pure) in the distinctive uniform worn by Guru Gobind Singh. He carries a ceremonial sword symbolizing his willingness to defend the faith against outside aggression.*

Above *Sikh elders transport the* Guru Granth Sahib *to the temple, where it is installed with great ceremony.*

The *Guru Granth Sahib*

Guru Gobind Singh, the tenth and last living guru, is regarded with almost as much veneration as the founder, Guru Nanak. He was responsible for two key developments that have shaped the Sikh identity to this day. The first was the foundation of the *Khalsa*—the community of "pure" Sikhs, who were prepared to die for their faith. They are baptized with holy water (*amrit*), given the name *Singh*, meaning "lion" (female members were called *Kaur* meaning "princess"), and told to wear a distinctive uniform that marked them out as brave soldier-saints. His second innovation was to place authority over the Sikh community, not in the person of a living guru, but in the Sikh holy scripture. From then on, it was known as the *Guru Granth Sahib*.

Left *The* Guru Granth Sahib, *also known as the* Adi Granth *(the first book), is the Sikhs' holiest scripture.*

SIKHISM'S HOLY CITY

Amritsar is the Sikh holy city in the state of Punjab in northwest India and Pakistan. It is here that the Golden Temple was completed in 1601, by the fifth guru, Guru Arjan. The Golden Temple, also known in Punjabi as the Harimandir Sahib (house of God), is Sikhism's holiest shrine. By day, it houses the holy scripture, the *Guru Granth Sahib.* At night, the scripture is stored in a nearby building, the Akal Takht. While the Golden Temple is devoted to worship, the Akal Takht, or seat of temporal power, is a kind of parliament and conference hall where political and social matters are discussed.

Daily worship at the Golden Temple starts at four o'clock in the morning—an hour before the *Guru Granth Sahib* is installed each day—and continues until midnight. Hymns (*kirtan*) from the scriptures are sung all day long, and the temple attracts a constant stream of visitors and pilgrims. During the early 1800s, the Temple's two upper stories were covered with gold leaf. The name by which it is known to foreigners, the Golden Temple, dates from this time.

"All creatures on their actions are judged in God's court, just and true."

Guru Granth Sahib

Although it is a focal point of worship, the Golden Temple is part of a much larger complex of guest houses, conference centers, dining halls, watchtowers, cloisters, and a museum. At the entrance to the Temple compound is a gateway called the Darshani Deorhi, above which are stored the golden spades that were used to dig the lake. In front of the gateway is a cardamom tree, where a small shrine marks the spot where Guru Arjan is believed to have sat while he supervised the excavation of the pool.

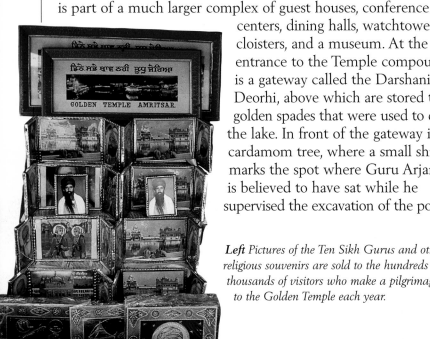

Left *Pictures of the Ten Sikh Gurus and other religious souvenirs are sold to the hundreds of thousands of visitors who make a pilgrimage to the Golden Temple each year.*

Left and below The Golden Temple, which by day houses the Sikh scripture, the Guru Granth Sahib, is Sikhism's holiest shrine. Visitors and pilgrims reach it by a 200-foot causeway built across the Lake of Immortality. Moving across the lake to the shrine is in itself a solemn act of worship.

The temple complex has been the scene of many conflicts throughout its history. In the 1700s, it witnessed frequent fighting between the Sikhs and the Moguls—Muslims from Afghanistan. The latest conflict was in 1984, when Indian security forces stormed the Golden Temple and shot dead a Sikh activist, the leader of a movement for Sikh independence. In the fighting that followed, the Akal Takht was virtually destroyed and had to be rebuilt. Later the same year, the Indian Prime Minister, Indira Gandhi, was assassinated in a retaliation that prompted a massacre of Sikhs and several years of fighting between the Indian authorities and Sikh separatists.

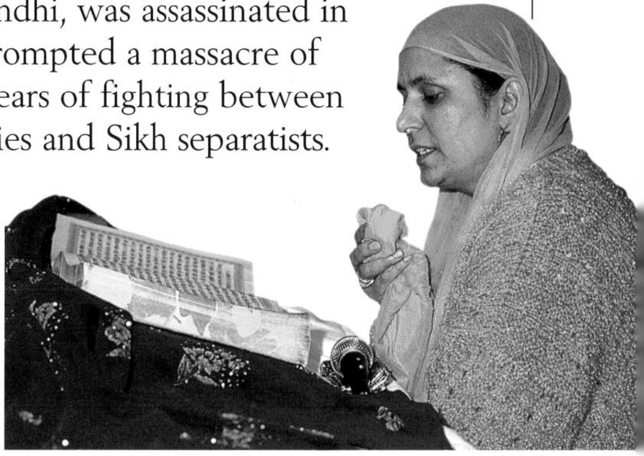

Right *A Sikh woman reads the holy scripture,* Guru Granth Sahib.

Life as a Sikh

The turban is the most distinctive feature of Sikh dress but it is only one element of the traditional customs and practices of the faith. When a man is initiated into the Khalsa (becomes a full member of the Sikh religion), he must wear the Five Ks—so-called because the Punjabi words describing them each begin with a "K." They are: *kesh*, uncut hair covered by the turban; the *kirpan*, a short sword symbolizing resistance against evil; the *kara*, a steel bracelet symbolizing faithfulness to God (originally protection for the sword arm); the *khanga*, a comb symbolizing personal hygiene; and the *kach*, knee-length breeches symbolizing purity. Meat slaughtered in the Muslim way along with tobacco and alcohol are forbidden, as are stealing, gambling, and unfaithfulness to one's marriage partner. Sikhs should get up early, bathe, then meditate on the name of God (*Nam*). Each day, they should read or recite from the scriptures and, if possible, join a congregation (*sangat*) at the temple (*gurdwara*) where they can listen to the words of the gurus and do charitable work.

At the center of temple worship is the Sikh holy scripture, the *Guru Granth Sahib*. Members of the congregation must kneel in its presence and approach it barefoot and with the head covered. On special occasions, a temple supervisor, or *Granthi*, may lead the worship, waving a type of fan or whisk (a *chauri*) over the text as he reads the words aloud. At the end of the recitation of hymns, the congregation joins in the collective prayer (*ardas*).

Above *At a Sikh wedding, the bride often wears traditional Punjabi red. Gifts of money are made to the couple, and passages from the* Guru Granth Sahib *are read out to bless the marriage.*

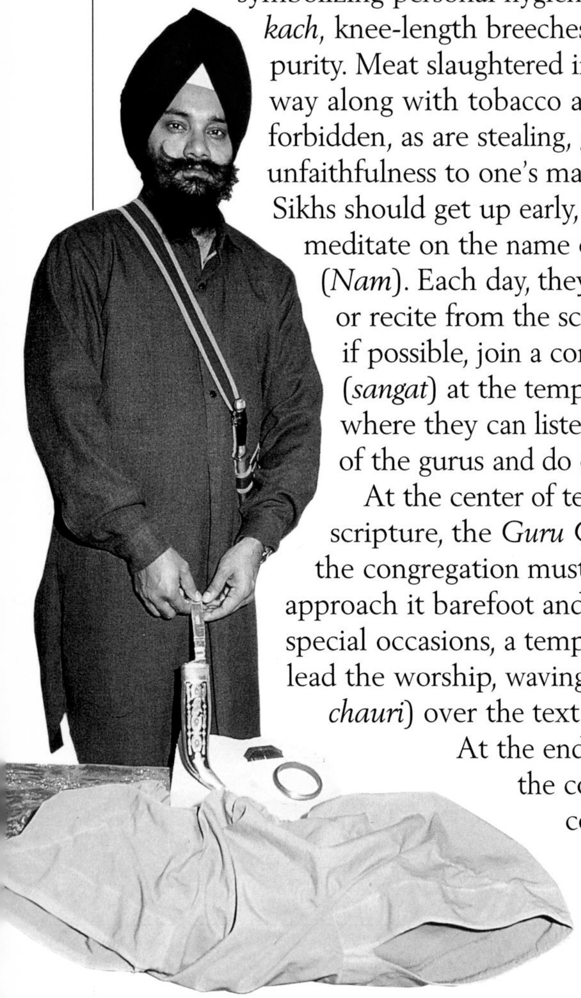

Left *This Sikh wears the traditional costume demonstrating the Five Ks—* kesh, kirpan, kara, khanga, *and* kach.

Right *The Khanda is a sign often used for Sikhism. The central, double-edged sword symbolizes belief in one god. The two outer blades represent spiritual and temporal power.*

The *Guru Granth Sahib* also plays a part in family ceremonies. For example, when naming newborn babies the book is opened at random and the first letter of the first hymn on that page is used as the first letter of the baby's name. At a marriage ceremony (*anand karaj*), the bride and groom walk around the holy book four times as a sign of its importance in their future life together. A section of the scripture known as the *Kirtan Sohila* is read at funeral services. The dead person is dressed in the traditional Five Ks and the body is cremated as soon as possible, usually on the day of death. To mark births, deaths, and marriages, Sikhs often hold an "*akhand path*," a continuous 48-hour reading of the *Guru Granth Sahib* timed to end at dawn on the day of the particular event being celebrated. Sikh festivals (*gurpurbs*) usually commemorate the birth or death of one of the Ten Gurus or an event associated with his life.

Right *This young girl wears traditional costume at the festival for Guru Gobind Singh's birthday.*

Sikh Festivals

December/January Guru Gobind Singh's birthday.

February **Hola Mohalla:** the fair in Anandpur in honor of Guru Gobind Singh.

April **Baisakhi:** a celebration of the foundation of the Khalsa.

August A celebration of the completion of the *Guru Granth Sahib*.

October Guru Nanak's birthday.
Diwali: a Hindu festival used by Sikhs to mark the release from prison of Guru Hargobind.

THE LIFE OF THE BUDDHA

Left *The Buddha is said to have attained* nirvana *beneath the Bodhi tree, or tree of enlightenment.*

There are many myths and legends surrounding the life of the Buddha, but most scholars accept that Buddhism's historical founder lived between 485 and 405 B.C. Siddhartha Gautama came from a prosperous family and led a privileged life. At the age of 29, he is said to have observed three things that prompted him to embark on his spiritual quest: illness; aging; and death and decay. Tradition has it that he met a holy man who, despite his poverty, was happy. At that moment, Siddhartha Gautama realized that life's pleasures are illusions, and that the only road to contentment lies in what is real and true. He decided to leave his home and devote himself to the quest for truth.

"I am is a vain thought. I am not is a vain thought. I shall be is a vain thought. I shall not be is a vain thought. Vain thoughts are a sickness. But after overcoming all vain thoughts one is called a silent thinker."

The words of the Buddha

The Four Noble Truths

At first he became an ascetic; meditating, fasting, and practicing severe exercises of self-denial that made his hair fall out and ruined his health, leaving him weak and emaciated. After six years he decided such extremes of self-discipline were unsatisfactory and the best route to enlightenment was along a path of moderation. One night, his life changed forever when, seated beneath a tree (later called the Bodhi tree, or tree of enlightenment), he began a deep and prolonged meditation. In the course of his meditation he attained a state of perfect knowledge and perfect peace (*nirvana*). This was the moment when he gained insight into The Four Noble Truths—the core of Buddhist teaching.

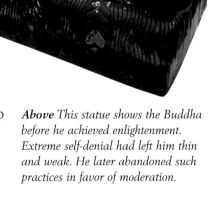

Above *This statue shows the Buddha before he achieved enlightenment. Extreme self-denial had left him thin and weak. He later abandoned such practices in favor of moderation.*

Right *The Buddha's teaching is often symbolized by a wheel (seen here in his left hand). In his first sermon in Benares, the Buddha declared that he was setting in motion "the wheel of* dharma.*"*

THE FOUR NOBLE TRUTHS

- All existence is unsatisfactoriness.
- Unsatisfactoriness is caused by the craving (*tanha*) for something permanent in the world when no such permanence exists.
- The cessation of unsatisfactoriness, *nirvana*, can be attained.
- *Nirvana* can be reached following The Noble Eightfold Path.

THE NOBLE EIGHTFOLD PATH

Each of these eight steps to *nirvana* contains the word *samma*, or right.
Right knowledge
Right attitude
Right speech
Right action
Right livelihood
Right effort
Right state of mind
Right concentration

Shortly after this he gathered around him five companions, who became his first disciples. Traveling around India for the next 45 years, he lived the life of a beggar and teacher. The Buddha died at the age of 80 in the town of Kushinagara. Among his last words to his followers were, "Do not cry. Have I not told you that it is in the nature of all things, however dear they may be to us, that we must part with them and leave them?"

The Development of Buddhism

After the Buddha's death, his followers decided to preserve his teachings. This was not easy because nothing had been written down—indeed, it was not until more than 350 years later that the first Buddhist writings appeared. To bring the master's ideas together, Buddhist monks held a council in Rajagriha and agreed that their conclusions should be reviewed 100 years later in Vesali. But it was the third Buddhist council, held at Pataliputta, that proved the most significant. Monks gathered to try to agree on the Buddha's message, and, though at first there was considerable agreement, there were also the first signs of a deep division.

Above *A page of the Chinese translation of the so-called* Diamond Sutta. *This version appeared in the* A.D. *800s and is the oldest printed book in the world. The* Diamond Sutta *belongs to the collection of* Mahayana *scriptures known as* The Perfection of Wisdom Suttas.

Two schools of thought

Out of this emerged two distinct forms of Buddhism—early and late. The only surviving school of early Buddhism is known as *Theravada*, and all later schools are collectively referred to as *Mahayana*. The main difference between early and late Buddhism is the interpretation of the various teachings. However, they also use different texts. *Theravada* means "the teaching of the elders." Its scriptures contain three sets of teachings that were originally written on palm leaves and stored in wicker baskets (hence the other name by which they are known—the *tripitaka*, or three baskets). The *Sutta Pitaka*, or "basket of doctrinal teachings," is believed to contain the teachings of the Buddha himself. The *Vinaya Pitaka*, or "basket of monastic disciplinary rules," contains more material about the Buddha and lays down the rules of discipline for the monastic community. The *Abhidhamma Pitaka*, or "basket of higher teaching," is for serious scholars. The *Mahayana* tradition, or "Great Vehicle," has its own texts, or *suttas*.

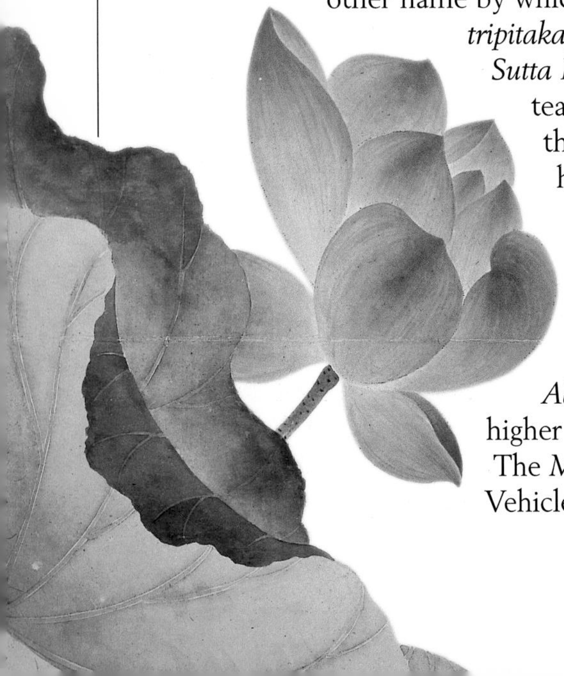

Left *The lotus flower, a water lily with its roots in the mud, features frequently in Buddhist imagery. It symbolizes the belief that enlightenment (the flower) can be achieved in the midst of human suffering (the mud and slime beneath the water).*

***Above** Buddhists believe that* stupas *(ancient burial mounds) contain relics of early Buddhist holy men, or even of the Buddha himself. Many* stupas*, like this one in Nepal, have become important places of pilgrimage.*

One of the distinctive features of *Theravada* Buddhism is the idea of the *arhat*. This is a person who has achieved enlightenment through the teaching of another enlightened being (a buddha). Theravadins believe that only monks can achieve such a state and so try to spend some of their lives in a monastery. Mahayana Buddhists, on the other hand, believe that everyone is capable of achieving enlightenment. They attach great importance to the concept of the *bodhisattva*, a semi-divine being who has achieved enlightenment, but who has voluntarily renounced *nirvana*, to stay in the world to help others. By the A.D. 1000s, Buddhism had declined in influence in India, but was flourishing in many other Asian countries.

"When I attain this highest perfect wisdom, I will deliver all sentient beings into the eternal peace of *nirvana*."

The Buddha's words, taken from the *Diamond Sutta*

TYPES OF BUDDHISM

Buddhism spread beyond India to central and southeastern Asia and adapted to the culture of the countries in which it took root. Different varieties of Buddhist practice emerged—*Mahayana* Buddhism, in particular, includes several distinctive traditions.

Above The 14th Dalai Lama, here receiving worshipers, fled from Tibet in 1959 because he and his followers feared persecution by the Chinese.

Chinese Buddhism

Buddhism arrived in China by A.D. 100 and was practiced alongside Confucianism and Taoism (*see pages 74–81*). By the A.D. 300s, many of the texts had been translated from Sanskrit into Chinese, and many of the *bodhisattvas* had their Chinese equivalents. For example, Avalokiteshvara, the Bodhisattva of Compassion, became Kuan Yin (believed to take the form of a young woman who is ready to help people in trouble).

Tibetan Buddhism

Tibet has its own forms of Buddhism, which combine magic and spirit worship with a type of *Mahayana* Buddhism known as *Vajrayana* ("the vehicle of the thunderbolt"). *Vajrayana* is based on ancient texts called *tantras* and involves ritual practices, such as meditation and chanting *mantras* (words believed to have powerful energies).

Of the many schools of Tibetan Buddhism, the best known is the Gelukpa tradition (also known as the Yellow Hats). This monastic tradition stresses the importance of living teachers (*lamas*) to instruct novices in the ways of Buddhist thought. The leader of this school is the Dalai Lama ("lama as great as the ocean"), who is believed to be a reincarnation of the Bodhisattva Avalokiteshvara. When the Dalai Lama dies, other lamas search for a child they believe to be the reincarnation of the "compassionate one," and he becomes the next Dalai Lama. Following their occupation of Tibet in 1951, the Chinese attempted to control the monasteries, and Tibetan Buddhism is still struggling to keep its traditions intact.

Left The wheel is an important symbol in Buddhism, as it suggests the cycle of birth, death, and reincarnation. The 12 spokes may also represent the Four Noble Truths and the Noble Eightfold Path.

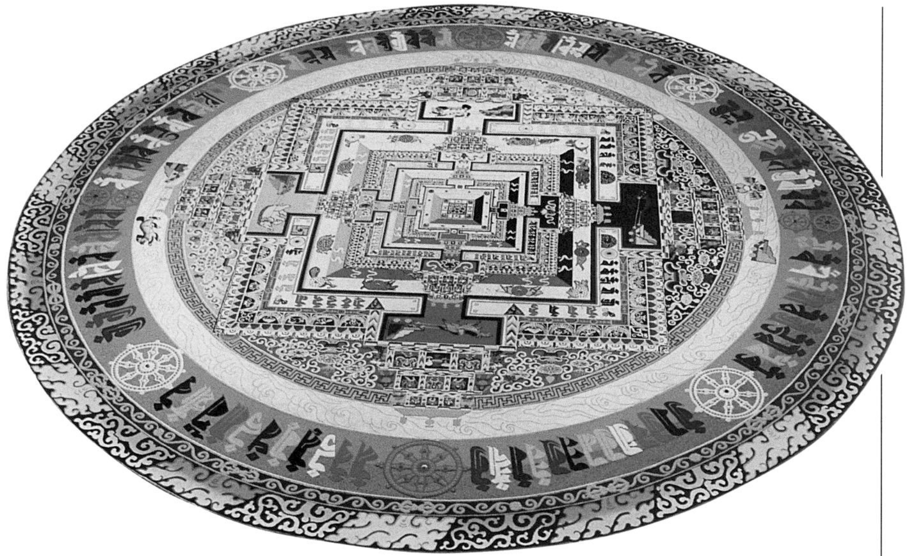

__Above__ Mandalas are maps of the cosmos. They are believed to possess spiritual energy and are used as an aid to meditation in Tantric Buddhism. They are painted, carved, or, as here, made out of sand.

Japanese Buddhism

Buddhism reached Japan in the A.D. 500s, arriving from China via Korea. The most popular school of Japanese Buddhism is *Jodo Shu*, or "Pure Land." This is based on a *Mahayana* text that tells of a Buddha called Amitabha (or Amida), who lives in a distant world known as the Pure Land. Faith in the Amida Buddha and meditation on his name will, it is believed, lead to rebirth in that heavenly land where *nirvana* can easily be reached. However, the school best known in the West is Zen, which derives its name from the Chinese *ch'an*, meaning "meditation." Zen concentrates on meditation and intuition above worship, and prefers study as a way of achieving sudden enlightenment (*satori*). Other means of achieving *nirvana* include *zazen* (sitting cross-legged in the lotus position) and answering a *koan*, or riddle. The purpose of these riddles (such as "What is the sound of one hand clapping?") is to surprise students into looking at things differently, and in doing so, to challenge the conventional patterns of thought that prevent them from achieving enlightenment.

__Left__ A Zen garden is often used in meditation. Its simple patterns of raked sand suggest the natural shapes of rivers, mountains, and waves.

Shinto Worship

Shinto worship (*matsuri*) is both public and private and revolves around the life-cycle events of a family or community. It is common, for example, for pregnant women to visit a shrine to ask for the safe delivery of their child. Thirty-two days after a male child is born (33 days for a girl), the baby is carried to the shrine by the mother or grandmother for a *hatsu miya-mairi*, or first shrine visit, and brought into the presence of the *kami* for a blessing. Later in childhood, the *shichi-go-san* (seven-five-three) festival is held. Parents with three- or seven-year-old sons, or five-year-old daughters, bring them to the shrine for a purification rite, or *harai*. During this service, a wand with paper streamers may be waved over the children's heads to remove bad influences from their lives and to purify them for the future.

Above *Shinto worshipers hang up a prayer board, or* ema, *outside a shrine and write their requests on it.*

Below *The* Tori no Ichi *festival was originally a celebration of the god of battle, but now celebrates good luck. Here, a man holds a lucky charm made of straw.*

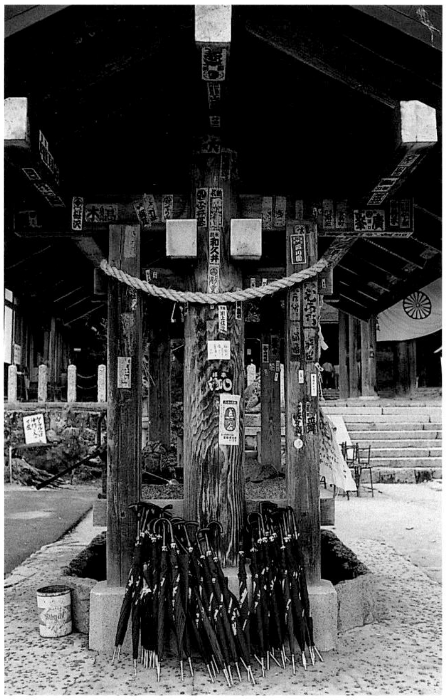

***Above** This shrine has a* shimenawa*— a thick rope threaded with folded white paper to denote a sacred space.*

Entering the shrine

Elaborate rituals surround entry to the shrine. It is approached through a *torii,* a wooden or stone archway that separates the outside world from the sacred space within. At the entrance is a trough of running water where worshipers wash their hands and rinse their mouths. Then they proceed to the prayer hall, or *haiden,* where the *kami* are alerted to their presence by two claps of the hands. After putting money into the offertory box, ringing a bell, and making a deep ritual bow to the *kami,* worshipers can offer their prayers. In one part of the shrine complex is a wall on which visitors can hang an *ema*. This is a five-sided wooden board on which worshipers write their requests, which may be anything from curing a disease or giving up smoking, to winning the lottery. At the New Year festival these prayer boards are burned to make room for the following year's prayers.

***Above** A priest burns the previous year's prayer boards in a ceremony at the Shinto Shrine in Ise, Japan.*

The *honden*

Beyond the *haiden* is the *honden,* the main hall where the *kami* live. Only priests may enter this space. During festival times, the image of the *kami* is taken out of the main shrine and placed in a *mikoshi,* or portable shrine. It is then paraded through the town so that the whole community can be blessed by the spirits. *Fudas,* or charms, are sold to help bring good luck and ward off evil spirits. These are then taken home and put on a *kami* shelf, where they remain for a year, protecting the family from misfortune.

Sometimes, if someone cannot go to a shrine, a priest goes out to offer prayers in the name of the *kami*. He might go to a construction site to purify it and to ask for the building (a bank, say, or the headquarters of an industrial corporation) to be blessed by the spirits' presence. Priests will even bless a new car in the hope that it will not be involved in an accident.

***Right** Children's Day takes place once a year in November at the Meiji Shrine, the most popular shrine in Tokyo. Parents bring their children to receive a blessing for the future.*

Taoist Practice

Taoists believe that an energy (*ch'i*) runs through the whole of creation. It is found in mountains and plains, in rivers and streams, in trees and flowers, in heaven and Earth, and, crucially, in human beings. Harnessing this vital energy harmoniously (with the correct balance of yin and yang) is the key to a long and ultimately happy life.

Above *It is common to see groups of people of all ages practicing* t'ai ch'i *in public places. This stylized series of exercises was originally a martial art and is practiced to harmonize the yin and yang forces in the human body, as well as to promote health and long life.*

Harmony and balance

To achieve harmony, certain Taoist groups have developed elaborate rituals involving meditation, chanting, physical exercise, and natural medicine. The mere chanting of certain Taoist texts is believed to bring about a physical and mental change in a person, promoting the harmony of yin and yang that is the goal of religious Taoism. When these forces are not in harmony, things start to go wrong. An imbalance of yin and yang, for example, is believed to be at the root of some diseases that can only be cured when the balance is restored. Destructive energy, often in the form of an unquiet spirit, is thought to be a result of excess yin.

Left *Taoist priests play an important role in Chinese communal worship. Their function is to perform the harmonizing rites that will ensure health and long life for the community.*

Achieving immortality
Whereas Confucians strive to become sages or wise people at the service of society, the Taoist strives to become an immortal (a *hsien*). Confucianism places greater emphasis on the organization of the ideal state than Taoism, which is more concerned with the individual and personal development. Some Taoists interpret the notion of immortality literally and go to great lengths to achieve it. In the past, stories circulated of secret rituals known only to a select group of devotees who drank herbal potions to become immortal. There were tales of supernatural feats of levitation where their bodies would rise up into the air by magic. Some of these Taoist societies still exist today.

Natural medicine
Most practicing Taoists do not go to such extremes. They believe the body is like the natural landscape, crisscrossed by invisible channels of vital energy that control bodily functions. At certain points along these channels, a little like floodgates along a canal, are points where the flow of energy can be interrupted and controlled in order to reestablish the correct combination of yin and yang. At these points, acupuncturists (traditional healers) insert fine needles to treat various ailments. Taoism says that nothing is fixed. Life is in constant flux and humanity should go with its flow.

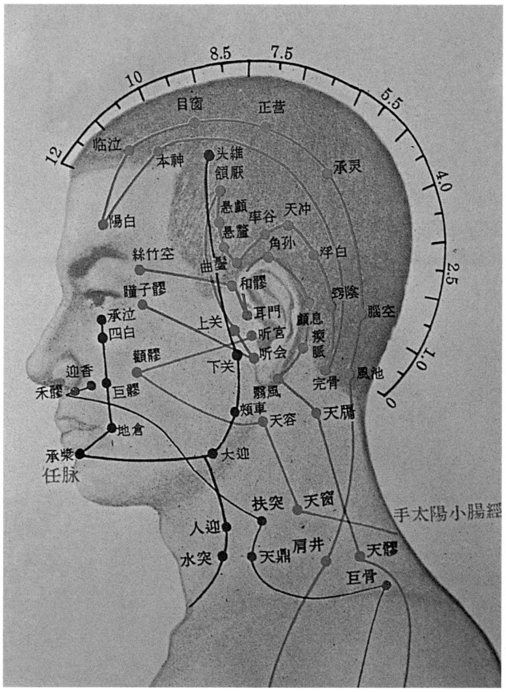

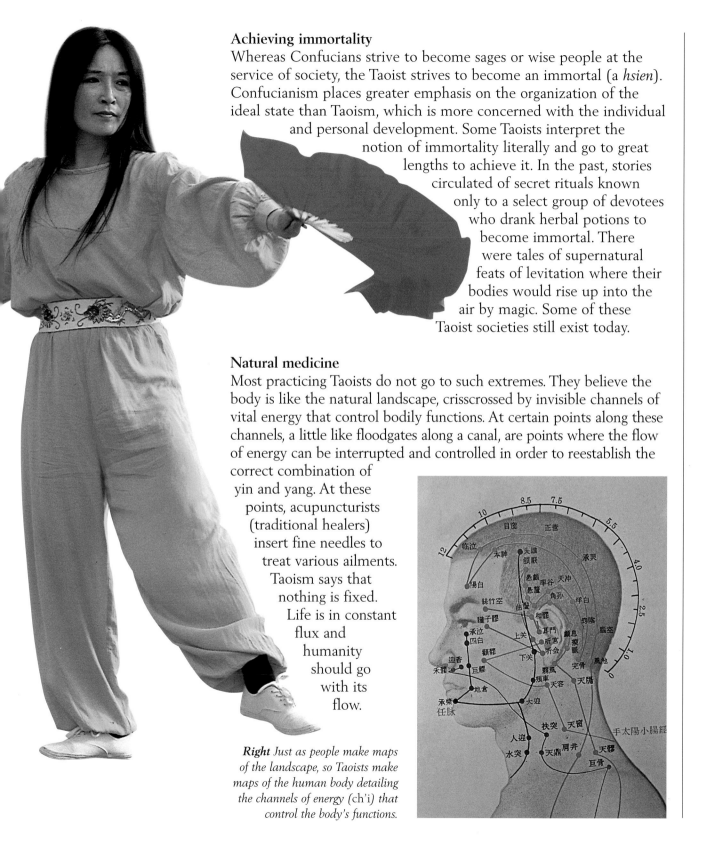

Right *Just as people make maps of the landscape, so Taoists make maps of the human body detailing the channels of energy (ch'i) that control the body's functions.*

GLOSSARY

Altar A table (often made from wood or stone) on which to make offerings to God or a god.

Amrit Sikh holy water.

Artifact An object.

Ascetic One who renounces earthly comforts and practices extreme self-discipline to concentrate on the spiritual life.

Ashrama In Hinduism one of the four stages of spiritual life.

Avatar In Hinduism a specific earthly manifestation of Vishnu, who has many forms.

Boddhisattva In Buddhism an enlightened one who has deliberately postponed *nirvana* to help others on their spiritual journey on Earth.

Brahman In Hinduism the supreme and eternal being of all Creation.

Brahmin A member of the Hindu priestly class.

Caste A class of person, especially in Hinduism.

Ch'i In Taoism the universal energy that flows through everything.

Deity A manifestation or form of God.

Dharma In Hinduism the eternal law of the universe. In Buddhism the teachings of the Buddha.

Diva In Hinduism a small devotional lamp that refers to the flame, rather than to the physical lamp.

Ema A Shinto prayer board.

Enlightenment In Buddhism, a state of perfect spiritual insight and understanding.

Five Ks The five badges of Sikh identity: *kesh*, uncut hair covered by the turban; *khanga*, the comb; *kirpan*, the short sword; *kara*, the bracelet; *kach*, knee-length breeches.

Gurdwara A Sikh temple.

Guru In Hinduism a wise teacher. Also in Sikhism one of the ten principal leaders of the faith.

Guru Granth Sahib Sikhism's holiest scripture that is revered as if it were a living guru. Also known as the *Adi Granth* (the First Book).

Honden The main hall of a Shinto shrine.

Hymn A sacred song.

Immortal Living forever.

Kami Shinto spirits inhabiting the natural world.

Karma In Hinduism the law of cause and effect. In Jainism the invisible matter preventing the soul from progressing.

Kaur A name, meaning "princess," given to fully initiated Sikh women.

Khalsa The community of fully initiated Sikhs.

Khanda The double-edged sword—symbol of Sikhism.

Kirtan Sanskrit word for glorification. Used by Hindus and Sikhs to describe gatherings for chanting of poetry and hymns. A Sikh hymn.

Koan A Zen Buddhist riddle designed to help people achieve enlightenment.

Kshatriyas The Hindu warrior caste.

Mahayana A later branch of Buddhism.

Mandir A Hindu temple.

Mantra In Buddhism and Hinduism a word or phrase repeated as part of meditation ("man" means mind, and "tra" means to release from).

Meditation Intense spiritual concentration.

Megalith A gigantic, prehistoric stone monument.

Moksha In Hinduism and Jainism release from the ongoing cycle of birth, death, and rebirth.

Monastery A community of religious men (monks).

Nam The Divine Name in both Sikhism and Hinduism.

Nirvana The release from all suffering and desire into a perfect spiritual state.

Pilgrimage A journey to a sacred site.

Prehistoric Belonging to a period before the existence of written records, approximately more than 5,000 years ago.

Prophet A teacher or interpreter of the will of God.

Puja Daily Hindu worship.

Reincarnation Rebirth of the soul into a new body.

Sacrifice A precious offering made to God or the gods.

Samsara In Hinduism the continual cycle of birth, death, and rebirth.

Sangat A congregation of Hindus or Buddhists.

Shrine A sacred building or place set aside to commemorate a holy person. Also a Shinto place of worship.

Shudras In traditional Hindu society the laboring or servant class.

Singh Meaning "lion," the name given to fully initiated Sikh men.

Tao "The way," the underlying harmony governing the universe.

Theravada The early branch of Buddhism.

Torii A stone or wooden arch at the entrance to a Shinto shrine.

Transcendence A state of being that goes beyond the material world into a higher realm of experience and consciousness.

Trinity A collection of three.

Vaishyas Hinduism's trading and farmer class.

Varnas In classical Hinduism the four classes of person.

Vedas Hinduism's earliest scriptures, made up of four sacred texts.

Yang The male principle, associated with heaven, heat, and light.

Yin The female principle, associated with Earth, darkness, and cold.

Yin* and *yang In Chinese philosophy opposite but complementary forces.

INDEX

Acknowledgments

The publisher would like to thank the following for permission to reproduce their material. Every care has been taken to trace copyright holders. However, if there have been unintentional omissions or failure to trace copyright holders, we apologize and will, if informed, endeavor to make corrections in any future edition.

Cover main and inset Corbis; 6tr Getty; 6br Getty; 7tl Corbis; 7b Corbis; 8bl Bridgeman Art Library/National Museum of India; 8–9 Roger Hutchins; 9tr C.M. Dixon; 10–11 Magnum Photos/Steve McCurry; 11tc Bridgeman Art Library; 11br Bridgeman Art Library; 12cl Bridgeman Art Library; 12–13 India Office Library; 14tr Bridgeman Art Library/British Library; 14cl Frank Spooner; 14br Bridgeman Art Library/Oriental Museum, Durham University; 15 Bridgeman Art Library/Victoria & Albert Museum; 16tr Hutchison Library/Liba Taylor; 16bTony Stone/Mark Lewis; 17tl Hutchison Library; 17bl Still Pictures/Sarvottam Rajkoomar; 18cl Robert Harding; 18br Hutchison Library/J. Horner; 19 Hutchison Library; 20tr Trip/H. Rogers; 20bc Robert Harding; 21t Michael Freeman; 21bl Magnum Photos/Raghu Rai; 22bl Magnum Photos/Raghu Rai; 22–23 Michael Freeman; 23tr Robert Harding/Jeremy Bright; 23br Format/Judy Harrison; 24bl Format/Judy Harrison, BL; 24–25 Panos/Liba Taylor; 25br Michael Freeman; 26tc Michael Freeman; 26cm Michael Freeman; 27 Bridgeman Art Library/Oriental Museum, Durham University; 28bl Bridgeman Art Library/Osaka Museum of Fine Arts; 28tr E.T. Archive/British Library; 29t Sygma; 30bl Trip/B. Vikander; 30–31 Magnum Photos/Raghu Rai; 31tr Magnum Photos/Ferdinando Scianna; 31bl Network/E. Grames/Bildenberg; 32tr Michael Freeman; 32b Michael Freeman; 33tl Trip/P.Rauter; 33bl Michael Freeman; 33cr Network/Gideon Mendel; 34bl Magnum Photos/Fred Mayer; 34–35 Hutchison Library/Robert Francis; 35br Magnum Photos/Bruno Barbey